D1121530

LET'S GET MOVING!

You Can Do
Yoga

Alix Wood

Gareth Stevens
Publishing

Please visit our website, **www.garethstevens.com**. For a free color catalog of all our high-quality books, call toll free 1-800-542-2595 or fax 1-877-542-2596

Library of Congress Cataloging-in-Publication Data

Wood, Alix.
You can do yoga / by Alix Wood.
 p. cm. — (Let's get moving!)
Includes index.
ISBN 978-1-4824-0292-6 (pbk.)
ISBN 978-1-4824-0294-0 (6-pack)
ISBN 978-1-4824-0291-9 (library binding)
1. Hatha yoga for children — Juvenile literature. 2. Yoga — Juvenile literature. I. Wood, Alix.
II. Title.
RA781.7 W66 2014
613.7—dc23

First Edition

Published in 2014 by
Gareth Stevens Publishing
111 East 14th Street, Suite 349
New York, NY 10003

© Alix Wood Books

Produced for Gareth Stevens by Alix Wood Books
Designed by Alix Wood
Art direction and content research: Kevin Wood
Editor: Eloise Macgregor
Consultant: Molly Robertson

Photo credits:
Cover, 1, 3, 4, 5, 6 top, 8, 9, 10, 11, 13, 16, 18 top, 22, 23 top, 27 bottom, 28, 29, 30 © Shutterstock; all other images © Greg Dennis

Acknowledgments
With grateful thanks to James Latus, Josh Latus, Storm Brennon, Kieron Turk, Will Ferris, Corie Stubbs, and Ellena Harrison

Printed in the United States of America

CPSIA compliance information: Batch #CW14GS: For further information contact Gareth Stevens, New York, New York at 1-800-542-2595.

All sports can be dangerous. Do not attempt any of the skills in this book without supervision from a trained adult expert.

Contents

Why Do Yoga?

Yoga has been practiced for thousands of years. It is believed to unite the mind, the body, and the spirit. Yoga helps you become more aware of your body's posture, alignment, and movement.

Yoga is a great way to get fit. It makes the body more **flexible** and helps you to relax. Practicing yoga can make you happier and feel peaceful, too. Yoga is thought to help improve your memory and concentration. Many schools now start the day with a yoga session to help concentrate their students' minds. Yoga is also believed to help with anxiety and depression, and help lower your blood pressure and your pulse rate.

Yoga is fun and great exercise.

4

In a yoga class, the students usually place their mats facing the front. Leave a little space around your mat so you have space to do the poses. The students often sit cross-legged waiting for class to start, or they do some gentle stretches. The teacher may start the class with a breathing exercise or **meditation**. This is followed by warm-up poses, more vigorous poses, then stretches and then final relaxation exercises.

Yoga classes may use rolled up blankets as props for some poses. Some classes use blocks and straps (below) as well. The blocks act as props, and the straps help in poses where you need to hold your feet, for example, but can't quite reach.

Wear stretchy exercise pants or shorts. A fitted T-shirt is best. Baggy T-shirts can slide up when you are upside down. You can usually rent yoga mats to start with. Yoga is usually done barefoot.

TRY THIS

Most yoga classes end a session by saying "namaste" which means "I bow to you" in Hindi.

Meditation

Meditation is an important part of learning yoga. You don't have to learn to meditate to enjoy yoga, but it is generally considered to be part of the experience.

Yoga means union. Meditation is a way for people doing yoga to unite their body and mind. Meditation improves your ability to focus on things, including your yoga. Benefits of meditation include a decrease in blood pressure, improved breathing, and a slower resting heart rate. Chemicals in the body that are associated with stress may get lower as well. Meditation is also believed to make you look younger!

You can meditate in any still position. Sitting is the most common posture. A simple cross-legged pose is good for beginners.

Many people like to meditate near the calming presence of water.

To try to meditate, create a peaceful atmosphere, and wear comfortable clothing. Concentrate on one thing, such as your breathing, a word, or sensations you feel in your body. If your thoughts start to wander, take them back to your object of focus. To prevent other thoughts coming into your mind, try looking at an object such as a candle. Once your mind is clear of thought, you will feel calm, yet aware. People say this feeling cannot be described by words.

This child's pose is physically relaxing and one of the best yoga poses for mental relaxation.

Breathing

Controlling your breathing is important during yoga. Breathing correctly brings more oxygen to the blood and the brain.

Yoga breathing techniques help increase your lung **capacity**. Just as with meditation, concentrating on your breathing develops your focus, too. It fights stress and relaxes the body. Breathing correctly during a pose is important. If your breathing isn't relaxed, your body can't relax into the pose. If your body isn't relaxed, your mind can't relax. And if your mind isn't relaxed, you can't draw the full benefits from your yoga.

Yoga breathing control is called *pranayama*. The breath sets the rhythm for the practice. When you **inhale**, move into pose. When you **exhale**, move out of it. Your movements should match your breath.

The following yoga breathing exercises can make you feel dizzy, so ask a friend to be with you when you try out these techniques. *Kapalabhati* is a cleaning breath. Breaths are short, rapid, and strong. The lungs work as a pump, creating pressure as they expel the air and remove waste from the air passages.

Take two normal breaths. Breathe in.

Breathe out, pulling in your **abdomen**. Repeat 20 times, emphasizing breathing out. Finally, breathe in fully and hold your breath for as long as you can. Slowly breathe out.

TRY THIS

Alternate nostril breathing helps both sides of the brain to function properly.

Hold your hand as shown in the picture. Inhale through your left nostril, closing the right with your thumb. Count to four. Hold your breath, closing both nostrils. Count to 16. Exhale through the right nostril, closing the left with the ring and little fingers. Count to eight. Inhale using the right nostril, keeping the left nostril closed with the ring and little fingers. Count to four. Hold your breath, closing both nostrils, and count to 16. Exhale using the left nostril, keeping the right closed with the thumb. Count to eight.

Relaxing Breathing

You can help get rid of stress using these yogic breathing techniques.

Our normal shallow breathing doesn't **oxygenate** the blood very well. Try this breathing technique. Sit comfortably in a chair. Close your eyes and picture a swan gliding peacefully across a crystal-clear lake. Now, like the swan, let your breath flow along in a long, smooth, peaceful movement. Inhale and exhale through your nose. If your nose is blocked, use your nose and mouth, or just your mouth. Inhale and exhale as deeply as you can, and repeat this 20 times. Then gradually let your breath return to normal. Take a few moments to sit with your eyes closed and notice how different you feel overall.

One method of breathing used in yoga is called *ujjayi* breathing. The breathing is quite noisy, which helps focus your attention on each breath. The breath is done through the nose. First fill your lower abdomen, then your lower rib cage, and finally your upper chest and throat. As the throat passage is narrowed, the passage of air creates a "rushing" sound.

Ujjayi breathing should sound like the ocean. The "ocean sound" is created by moving the **glottis** as the air passes in and out.

Seated Exercises

Yoga isn't all about tying yourself in complicated knots. There are some simpler seated poses that are very good at improving your strength and flexibility.

This seated twist pose stretches your shoulders, hips, and back. It helps increase circulation and tones the abdomen. If you find this too hard, make it easier by keeping your bottom leg straight and place both hands on your raised knee. If your lower back rounds forward, sit on a folded blanket.

Seated Twist

- Sit on the floor with your legs extended.
- Cross your right foot over the outside of your left thigh. Bend your left knee. Keep your right knee pointed toward the ceiling.
- Place your left elbow to the outside of your right knee and your right hand on the floor behind you.
- Twist right as far as you can, moving from your abdomen. Keep both sides of your bottom on the floor. Stay for 1 minute.
- Switch sides and repeat.

This boat pose is great at exercising your stomach muscles and helps your balance.

Boat Pose

Sit with your legs out in front of you. Lean back and bend your knees, lifting your legs off the floor. Lean back further. Hold your thighs with your hands and pull in your lower back. Stretch your arms to the front, with your palms facing your body. After 5 to 10 breaths, slowly straighten your legs. Your feet should be higher than your head. Hold the pose for 5 to 10 breaths, then slowly release.

TRY THIS

Crossed legs and the Lotus Position

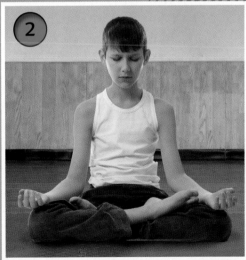

A cross-legged position is a good way to meditate and is a good way to sit in between poses in class.

To do a lotus, start cross-legged. Place one foot on the thigh, sole upward. Slowly try to lift the other foot, and place it on the other thigh.

Standing Poses

Standing poses help open up your chest and shoulders and help you build long, lean, strong arms and legs.

Doing a tree pose helps you with your balance and focus. Try it on both legs.

1. Stand with your arms at your sides.

2. Shift your weight onto your right leg and place the sole of your left foot inside your right thigh, keeping your hips facing forward.

3. Once balanced, bring your hands in front of you in a prayer position, with your palms together.

4. On an inhalation, extend your arms over your shoulders, palms separated and facing each other. Stay for 30 seconds.

5. Repeat the pose using the other leg.

The warrior pose is great for leg strength. It's important to keep your body straight over your hips.

Start by doing a low lunge, with your feet far apart. Bend your front knee.

Roll your back heel to the ground. Drop your shoulders and turn them parallel to your mat.

Reach your arms out, palms down, parallel to the ground. Keep your body vertical over your hips, with your front knee directly over your ankle.

Gaze out over your right hand. Hold the pose for 1 minute. Then try doing it on the other side.

Warrior and Triangle

Yoga doesn't just involve separate poses. Part of the workout you get is from moving from one pose to another.

There are several different warrior poses. You can try moving through them all. The pose on the right is called warrior I. Remember to inhale as you move into a pose, and exhale as you move out of it.

TRY THIS

Try this variation of warrior pose, warrior III.

Start from warrior pose, then hold both arms up, palms together. Lean forward and exhale. Lift your back foot and straighten your leg.

16

The triangle pose will help expand your shoulders and chest. This pose increases flexibility in your hip and neck joints. It also stretches the muscles in your spine, calves, and thighs.

Start from a warrior position.

Straighten your front leg, and follow your front hand forward, down to your shin or the floor.

Reach your top arm straight up, and bring your body and legs in the same line.

Arm Balances

This pose is called the downward dog. It is usually one of the first poses you will learn in a yoga class.

Downward dog uses the strength of your arms and legs to evenly stretch your spine. It stretches your hips, hamstrings, and calves. It opens your chest and shoulders and tones your arms and abdominals. It even tones your hands and feet, preparing you for standing poses and arm balances.

Start on your hands and knees, with your shoulders over your wrists, and your toes tucked.

Make a tall "V" shape by lifting your hips straight up, sinking upper chest and shoulders, and relaxing down the backs of your legs into your heels.

(1)

The plank builds arm and abdomen strength. You might find your arms shaking as you practice it at first.

The Plank
Start on your hands and knees, shoulders directly over your wrists.

(2)

Tuck your toes, extend your legs, and walk your feet back until your shoulders, hips, and ankles form a straight line.

TRY THIS

Stop your plank from sagging by inhaling to pull your abdomen in and straighten your lower back.

The Sideways Plank
From a plank, lift your hips up and shift your weight onto one hand. Roll your whole body to that side. Your shoulders, hips, and ankles should be in one straight line. Reach your top arm straight up.

19

The Crow

The crow builds strength in your arms, inner thighs, and abdomen. It looks really cool, too!

In the beginning, the crow posture can be painful for the wrists of some people. To make it easier, try shifting your weight forward until you feel some pressure on your wrists, and then practice lifting one foot and then the other off the ground until your wrists build up strength to lift both feet off the ground together.

Squat with your feet apart. Put your palms on the ground under your shoulders. Bend your arms slightly, and squeeze your knees firmly around your elbows or upper arms.

Rock your weight forward into your hands, coming up high on your toes. Lift your feet off the ground.

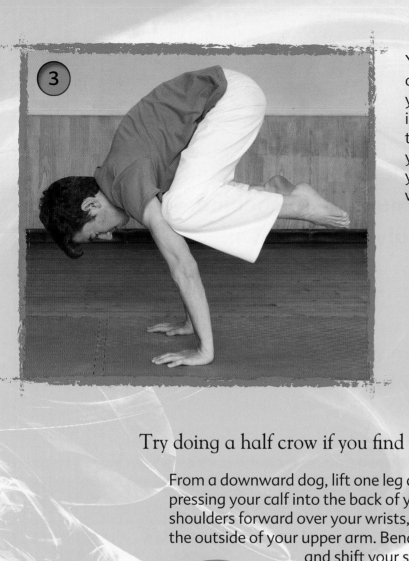

Your feet will lift easily off the ground when your weight is more in front of your hands than behind them. Lean your shoulders out past your wrists to shift your weight forward.

Try doing a half crow if you find the crow too difficult.

From a downward dog, lift one leg and bend your knee, pressing your calf into the back of your thigh. Roll your shoulders forward over your wrists, and bring your knee to the outside of your upper arm. Bend your elbows slightly and shift your shoulders forward to bring your back foot off the ground.

Floor Poses

Floor poses can be a great opportunity to leave the stress and trauma of life behind. One of them simply involves lying down!

It's called the corpse pose for a reason. It gives your body and mind a rest, surrendering and letting go of control. The corpse pose relaxes your central nervous system and calms your mind.

The Corpse Pose

Lie on your back with your knees bent. Lift your hips off the floor and lengthen your spine along the floor. Then drop your hips down again. Straighten your legs and let your feet fall out naturally to the sides. Slide your shoulders away from your ears and tuck your shoulder blades under you. Stretch out your arms and rest them loosely away from your body.

Let your head feel heavy. Breathe naturally in and out through the nose. Fill your throat, chest, and abdomen with every inhale. Exhale fully. Relax your eyes and focus on the inside of your forehead between your eyebrows. Feel a sense of stillness and calm. Stay for 5 to 30 minutes.

In child's pose you can hold your arms out to the front like this, or drape them alongside your legs.

Meditate!

The child's pose is not only physically relaxing. It's mentally relaxing, too. Try meditating in child pose.

The Child's Pose

Kneel on the floor, knees slightly apart and big toes touching. Lean forward until your forehead touches the floor. Let your face, neck, and shoulders relax. Breathe deeply into the abdomen. Release all tension away from the body as you sink deeper into the pose with each breath. Let your arms drape along your sides, palms up, or place them palms down in front of you.

The Pigeon

Begin in a push-up position, with your palms under your shoulders. Place your left knee on the floor near your shoulder with your left heel by your right hip. Lower down to your forearms. Bring your right leg down with the top of your foot on the floor. Stay on your forearms, or if you're more flexible, lower to floor and extend your arms in front of you, like in this picture.

Cobras and Bridges

Both of these poses exercise your spine and chest. The bridge strengthens your legs. The cobra is great for building arm strength, too.

The Cobra

Lie face down on the floor with your hands just in front of your shoulders. Your legs should be extended with the tops of your feet on the floor. Push strongly down with your pelvis and push up using your thumbs and index fingers. Raise your chest. Feel the power and stretch in your lower back.

Is it a Cobra or an Upward Facing Dog?

These two yoga poses look identical. The difference is where the power is coming from. In upward facing dog, the strength is in the shoulders, and the rest of body falls away. In cobra the power is in the lower back, the arms are merely props.

To do a King cobra, try to raise your legs to touch your head.

The bridge is called *Chatush Padasana*, which means "four foot pose." Your weight should be distributed evenly between your feet and shoulders, as if you had four feet.

1 Lie flat on your back. Bend your knees straight up, bringing your heels just behind your hips. Exhale and lift your hips up to knee height.

2 Grasp your ankles or **interlace** your fingers with your arms straight. Squeeze your shoulder blades together.

TRY THIS

If you find a bridge difficult, try using straps and blocks to help you achieve this pose.

The Hard Stuff

Although the main mission of yoga is balance, it can seriously challenge your strength and flexibility, too.

Headstands can be very challenging. They require great core strength and courage. Headstands are great for focus, calming the mind, increasing circulation, and aiding the nervous system. Muscular bodies can find headstands hard. Some very fit people have tight hamstrings, shoulders, and backs.

1 Make sure the space around you is safe if you fall. Get on your hands and knees.

2 Lower your forearms to the ground. Position your elbows under your shoulders.

3 Clasp your fingers together behind your head. Put the top of your head on the ground.

4 Walk your feet toward you until your hips are over your head. Lift one leg, then the other until both are straight up in the air.

Getting up is the tricky part. Try just lifting one leg at first and bending your knee so your calf is touching your thigh.

The aim of a wide-legged standing forward bend is to fold forward from the hips so you stretch your hamstrings without straining your back.

Stand with your feet apart, hands on your hips. Lift up tall, and then fold slowly over your legs. Place your hands on the floor, shoulder-width apart. Bring your head toward the floor. Bend your elbows.

Try This

If you get flexible enough, try this standing forward bend. Stand with feet slightly apart. Exhale and bend forward from the hip joints, not the waist. Try and touch your palms to the floor. Press your heels firmly into the floor.

If this is too difficult, you can try a half forward bend instead. Bend from the hips and touch the floor by your toes with your fingertips.

This pose is called the side extended hand to big toe pose! The pose helps with steadiness and poise.

Keeping your right leg straight, grasp your left big toe with your left first two fingers. Extend your left leg straight out to the side. Extend your right arm to the side for balance. Straighten both legs. Level your hips. Keep your body upright. Lift and broaden your chest. Exhale and bend the left leg to bring the leg down. Repeat on the other side.

To help you, try using yoga straps and a chair to support your leg once you raise it.

TRY THIS

If you can't manage the yoga pose, try the hand position. It is called *gyan mudra*, and is thought to bring peace and spiritual progress. Connect your thumb and forefinger tip to tip. The other fingers are straight but relaxed.

Pressure between the thumb and forefinger should be light.

If you managed to do the lotus position on page 13, you could try this elevated lotus.

Once you are in the lotus position, place your palms on the ground next to your hips. Gradually and smoothly raise your body above ground level so that your entire body weight rests on the palms of your hands. Lower your body and exhale. Your arms may tremble at first, but keep practicing and this will stop.

Be careful as this position requires flexible hips and legs. Don't hurt yourself.

This scorpion pose is a very advanced yoga pose. It can only be achieved after years of practice and discipline. Do not attempt this pose until your yoga teacher tells you that you are ready for it! The scorpion pose needs perfect balance and flexibility.

the scorpion pose

Glossary

abdomen The part of the body between the chest and the hips.

alignment The proper adjustment of parts in relation to each other.

capacity The ability to hold or contain.

exhale To breathe out.

flexible Capable of being bent.

glottis The long opening between the vocal cords in the larynx.

incense Material used to produce a fragrant odor when burned.

inhale To breathe in.

interlace To unite or cross as if you are lacing your fingers together.

meditation To spend time in quiet thinking.

oxygen A colorless, tasteless, odorless gas which forms about 21 percent of the atmosphere.

oxygenate To combine or supply with oxygen.

posture The position of one part of the body with relation to other parts. The general way of holding the body.

For More Information

Books

Chryssicas, Mary Kaye. *Breathe: Yoga For Teens.* New York, NY: DK Publishing, 2007.

Tieck, Sarah. *Yoga.* Minneapolis, MN: ABDO Publishing Company, 2013.

Websites

American Yoga Association
www.americanyogaassociation.org/general.html
Useful information about yoga, with links to history, teachers, and diet information.

Yoga for Beginners
www.yogaforbeginners.com
A website full of information about yoga, including how to get started, how to do the postures, the breathing, and meditation techniques.

Index